# The Airbnb Blueprint
## Building Wealth Through Short-Term Rentals

# Table of Contents

# Chapter 1. Introduction

Welcome to a world brimming with exciting opportunities and incredible financial potential! Get ready to journey through the lucidly outlined pages of "The Airbnb Blueprint: Building Wealth Through Short-Term Rentals" special report. This is not an abstract compilation of intricate jargon but a friendly walk through the lucrative world of short-term rental business. We delve into a comprehensive exploration of the strategies, practical tips, and success stories that could catapult you into a thriving short-term rental entrepreneur. By grasping the practical information furnished in this report, you'll not only be able to understand the dynamics of the Airbnb business but also chart a compelling course towards sustainable wealth creation. So, strap in as we uncover the keys to unlocking your financial future!

# Chapter 2. Understanding the Airbnb Model

Airbnb, a true embodiment of the Share Economy, has transformed the landscape of the lodging industry since its inception. Despite its relatively short duration in the market, it has produced a paradigm shift, demonstrating impressive growth, and amplifying global reach through its innovatively designed business model.

## 2.1. Foundation of Airbnb

Airbnb was founded in 2008 by Brian Chesky, Joe Gebbia, and Nathan Blecharczyk. The genesis of Airbnb is etched in an endeavor undertaken by the founders to pay their rent. They rented out three air mattresses in their living room and provided breakfast, an idea which paved the foundation for Airbnb, a blend of "Air Bed and Breakfast".

Airbnb's allure lies not just in its rental services but the experience it offers. The platform allows homeowners or 'hosts' to rent out their homes, apartments, or rooms to people or 'guests' who seek unique, affordable, and comfortable accommodations. It does not own any of the listed properties; it serves as an intermediary providing a robust platform facilitating the interaction between hosts and guests.

## 2.2. Understanding the Business Model Canvas

As we delve deep into understanding Airbnb's model, it is beneficial to view it through the lens of the Business Model Canvas. This strategic tool allows for a structured analysis of the business model components, painting an informative picture of how Airbnb generates value.

**Customer Segments**: Airbnb's customer base is segmented into two interdependent segments: the hosts who provide the accommodations and the guests who need them. The model relies on these two distinct yet intrinsically linked segments for operations and revenue flow.

**Value Proposition**: For hosts, Airbnb provides an opportunity to monetize their property and decide the parameters of the rental agreement. For guests, it offers a wide range of unique and affordable accommodations complete with personalized experiences.

**Channels**: Airbnb's platform serves as the primary medium of interaction, transaction, and communication. It promotes properties through its website and mobile app, and marketers use SEO, social media platforms, and other digital channels to reach an extensive audience.

**Customer Relationship**: The relationship is maintained mainly via the digital platform and is self-serve. However, Airbnb provides assistance through customer service channels in case of disputes or challenges.

**Revenue Streams**: Airbnb's primary revenue stream comes from commission-based income. Fees from hosts and guests, including service fees and commissions, constitute the platform's revenue.

**Key Activities**: Airbnb's key activities revolve around platform maintenance, customer service, marketing, and importantly, ensuring trust and security within its ecosystem.

**Key Partnerships**: Partnerships play an integral role in Airbnb's business model. These include property owners, photography services, cleaning services, insurance companies, and local government bodies.

**Key Resources**: Airbnb's primary resources are its proprietary platform, its customer base, brand reputation, and partnerships.

**Cost Structure**: The principal costs for Airbnb are platform maintenance, marketing, administration, and legal expenses.

# 2.3. Dissecting Airbnb's Revenue Model

Airbnb's revenue system thrives on a commission-based model. It charges both the hosts and guests, cleverly ensuring a continual income stream.

Hosts and guests are charged a service fee calculated on a percentage basis of the overall booking cost. The fee for hosts ranges from 3% to 5% whereas guests are charged anywhere from 0% to 20% based on the reservation subtotal.

Apart from this, Airbnb also offers a Plus program designed to highlight top-tier listings. Hosts pay a non-refundable application fee and potentially added costs for a professional photographer to picture their space.

Airbnb's latest addition, the Experiences feature, allows hosts to generate income by designing and offering personalized tours, cooking classes, or other unique experiences for guests. The company charges a 20% service fee on all Experiences bookings.

# 2.4. Trust & Security: Foundation Blocks

Airbnb's success hinges on its ability to maintain trust and security within its ecosystem. A robust user verification system, including government IDs, phone numbers, and email addresses, is installed to ensure user authenticity.

Similarly, Airbnb has launched a 'Host Guarantee Program', providing protection of up to $1,000,000 to hosts for damages that occur during stays. Additionally, the site's review and rating system allows for past behavior tracking, positively motivating users to maintain their reputation.

In conclusion, Airbnb represents a carefully calibrated model that capitalizes on the concept of shared economy. It's clear that element of trust and effective management underscore Airbnb's success. Understanding the facets of this novel lucrative system can guide you in building a successful property rental business, all while reveling in the joy of sharing your space with the world.

# Chapter 3. Sourcing Properties for Short-term Rentals

What sets a thriving Airbnb business apart is often the quality of properties in your portfolio. A strategic approach to sourcing properties is thus critical. Let's start by identifying a set of factors that could guide us through this process.

## 3.1. Criteria for Sourcing Properties

Of paramount importance are location and market dynamics. You must choose locations that tourists, business travelers, or individuals looking for short-term rentals find attractive. Depending on the demographic you are targeting, the 'ideal location' might differ. For a young, solo traveler, a condominium in the city might be a perfect choice. For families, a house near amusement parks or beaches might be more appropriate. Research on popular destinations, trending client demands, economic changes, and local regulations should inform your decision.

Understand the type of properties that deliver lucrative returns in your selected market. Are they small apartments, cottages, or large family homes? Here, both the initial investment and ongoing operational costs are to be factored in. A practical tactic could be to first venture into properties that require lower initial investments. As your business grows, gradually diversify.

A well-maintained property with modern amenities and aesthetic appeal can yield higher occupancy rates. Look for properties where you can make cosmetic enhancements or minor renovations to boost the property's charm. Also, consider proximity to popular attractions, availability of public transport, and neighborhoods' safety.

## 3.2. Finding Potential Properties

Once you have defined your criteria, it's time to find potential properties. A good place to start is property listing websites. Websites like Zillow, Realtor.com, Redfin, etc. offer comprehensive insights on properties, neighborhoods, and property prices. Public property auctions and local real estate meetups can also present exciting opportunities.

For off-market properties, collaborate with local real estate agents who possess deep knowledge about the local market. They can help you uncover less publicized dealings or those on the verge of hitting the market—giving you an edge in competitive markets.

## 3.3. Conducting Property Evaluations

When a potential property is identified, thorough evaluation is necessary. Begin with the financial considerations: price, potential rental income, operational costs, ROI, and break-even timing. This will highlight the property's feasibility.

Inspect the property meticulously. Look for existing defect, potential risks, necessary repairs, or areas for enhancements. Involve a professional property evaluator if required. Note that unappealing properties might bring down the rates and reputation of your Airbnb listing, thereby affecting your overall portfolio.

Apart from structural aspects, also consider the visual appeal. Online platforms like Airbnb thrive on photographs. A property with scenic views or vintage architectural charm might attract more bookings.

# 3.4. Negotiating the Purchase

Negotiations are a critical part of property sourcing. Aim for a win-win situation where you secure a reasonable deal, and the seller also feels satisfied. Engage a property lawyer to ensure that the property title is clear of any legal issues.

Look for ways to sweeten the deal for the seller. Quick closures, instant cash payment, or an agreement to conduct any impending repairs post-closing might appeal to sellers.

# 3.5. Closing the Deal and Onboarding the Property

Finally, once the negotiations are successful, close the deal. Your attorney and bank should handle the legalities and financial transactions.

After gaining ownership, start with minor enhancements, if needed, to increase appeal. Register the property on Airbnb, get professional photos taken, and create an attractive listing. Congratulations, you are now ready to welcome your guests!

In conclusion, sourcing properties for short-term rentals requires thorough analysis, calculated decisions, rigorous property evaluation, and negotiating skills. However, the efforts invested in sourcing the right properties will undoubtedly pay off in the long run and pave the way to your Airbnb success.

# Chapter 4. Legal Aspects of the Short-term Rental Business

As you embark on your adventure in the booming short-term rental market, understanding the legal implications is crucial to your success. One wrong step could result in hefty fines, litigation, or even the closure of your business. This in-depth examination of various legal aspects is designed to ensure that you navigate your business with confidence, innovation, and most importantly, adherence to the law.

## 4.1. Understanding Zoning Laws

Zoning laws, typically established by local governments, dictate how certain areas or zones of a community can be used. These have a direct bearing on your short-term rental business. To operate within the law, it would be savvy to research the zoning regulations specific to your area. Restrictions may prevent the operation of an Airbnb, particularly if the zone is designated for strictly residential purposes. Understanding and adhering to these zoning principles can make a significant difference in your entrepreneurial journey.

## 4.2. Short-term Rental Regulations

Distinctions between short-term rentals and traditional rentals are recognized by many cities and states. Therefore, it is incumbent upon you, the potential host, to understand these regulations. They may dictate the maximum number of days a property may be rented each year or even the types of property suitable for this type of activity. Some places, such as New York City, have strict rules about renting out entire homes or apartments, while others, like Austin, Texas, are more liberal.

## 4.3. Licensing and Permits

In some cities, you'll need a permit or license to operate a short-term rental business. Be sure to explore all necessary compliance measures before embarking on your venture. The acquisition of all relevant permits can ensure the legality and protection of your business, significant aspects in guaranteeing sustainable success. Remember, violating rental regulations can result in fines and other legal consequences.

## 4.4. Health, Safety, and Insurance Requirements

The safety and well-being of your guests are paramount. Hence, it's necessary to stay abreast of any health and safety regulations applicable to your Airbnb. For example, do you need to install fire alarms, emergency exit signs, or first aid kits? Understand any potential health inspection requirements or standards that you must meet. Further, acquiring the right insurance coverage is a failsafe step to protect your property and guests. Check with your current provider about a policy that covers short-term rentals, or consider Airbnb's Host Protection Insurance.

## 4.5. Taxes on Short Rental Business

Just as with any other business, short-term rentals are subject to taxation. Income earned from your Airbnb should be reported according to your local and national tax regulations. You might be able to offset some of these obligations with deductions for cleaning, repairs, or Airbnb service fees. You may also be responsible for collecting and remitting occupancy taxes on behalf of your guests. It is prudent to consult with a tax advisor to get a handle on these aspects.

# 4.6. Handling Disputes and Legal Claims

In running a short-term rental, disputes can arise - conflicts with guests, neighbors, or even the homeowner's association. Understanding local laws and having a well-written rental agreement can help to avoid, or at least manage, such situations. Sometimes, legal claims could arise due to property damage, personal injuries, or disturbances. Having sound legal counsel on your team could be an invaluable resource at such moments.

# 4.7. Creating a Solid Rental Agreement

An effective short-term rental agreement outlines the terms and conditions of your rental, rules, cancellation policy, and more. It offers a clear mutual understanding between you and your guests. Further, it serves as a legal tool in case of disputes or unmet expectations. While standard rental agreement templates can be found online, customized contracts usually serve hosts better and are often worth the small investment.

As we wrap up this chapter, remember that this is a high-level view of a complex domain. Each area mentioned here deserves your attention and understanding to ensure that you can navigate the legal waters of the short-term rental business. You don't need to be an expert on every clause in the housing law, but you should know enough to protect your interests and run your short term rental within legal bounds, and when in doubt, to seek professional help. As the saying goes - failing to prepare is preparing to fail, and in this business, preparation means understanding the legal specs pertinent to your venture.

# Chapter 5. Effective Property Management Strategies

Managing short-term rentals can be a rewarding albeit challenging endeavor. The triumph lies in the attentiveness to detail, effective planning, and prioritizing customer experience. Today, we will take you on a comprehensive journey to unpack proven strategies of property management. These tips and tricks will assist you in creating a prosperous Airbnb business.

## 5.1. Understanding Your Guests

The first crucial step in managing your property effectively is understanding who your guests are. Renters on Airbnb are diverse, ranging from business travelers, couples on a romantic getaway, families on vacation, to solo adventurers.

Identify your target market and tailor your services accordingly. For example, business travelers might appreciate a quiet workspace with a strong internet connection, while families may need kid-friendly amenities. Gathering insights and feedback from your guests will help you understand their preferences better, which in turn helps you offer a service that matches their needs and expectations.

## 5.2. Setting Up Your Property

One of the vital aspects of property management is setting up your property for success. Here are some key facets to consider:

- Location: The locale of your property can greatly influence how desirable your listing is. Proximity to city centers, popular tourist areas, business hubs, and local amenities like transportation, restaurants, and shopping centers play a significant role.

- Amenities: Offering the right amenities can set your property apart. Essentials such as Wi-Fi, clean linens, a fully equipped kitchen, air conditioning, washing machine, and dryer are all desirable features. Add extras such as board games, books, a premium coffee maker, or even a hot tub, to give your property a unique selling point.

- Special Requirements: Consider potential special requirements your guests might have. If the property is not on the ground floor, is there an elevator? Is it equipped to cater to guests with disabilities?

- Decor: The appearance of your property greatly affects booking rates. Opt for comfortable, practical, and appealing decor that makes guests feel at home.

## 5.3. Rules and Regulations

It is vital to establish clear rules for your property right from the start. Some of these rules may pertain to smoking or pet policies, the maximum number of guests, partying, and noise restrictions. Always communicate these rules clearly to your guests to prevent any conflicts.

Complying with regulations is equally important. Ensure you have necessary permissions, and you're up-to-date with local tax laws. Failing to abide by these rules could result in fines, or in severe cases, would lead to the discontinuation of your property rental.

## 5.4. Optimal Pricing Strategies

Pricing is one of the most significant aspects of property management. It's critical to balance between remaining competitive and maximizing your profits. Analyze your local market, take into consideration seasonal demand, and adjust your pricing accordingly. Using dynamic pricing tools can also help optimize your revenue per booking.

## 5.5. Delivering Excellent Customer Service

A critical component of successful property management is providing top-notch customer service. Respond promptly and professionally to inquiries and complaints. Also, ensure that the property is clean and ready for the guest's arrival. Offer local insights, and if possible, provide your guests with a small welcome gift to enhance their experience.

## 5.6. Using Technology to Your Advantage

Deploying technology can aid in managing your property more efficiently. Automation tools can help with scheduling cleaning services, sending reminders to guests, managing bookings, calculating optimal pricing, and much more. Additionally, using keyless entry systems or smart home devices can improve the guest experience.

## 5.7. Handling Damages and Disputes

Even when rules are clearly communicated, damages can occur, and disputes could arise. It's crucial to handle these situations with grace. Work out a resolution strategy that protects your interests, maintains a positive guest relationship, and adheres to Airbnb's policies.

## 5.8. Conclusion

Effective property management necessitates an understanding of your customer's needs, cleverly marketing your property, navigating rules and regulations, pricing effectively, providing top-notch customer service, leveraging technology, and adept handling of any eventualities. It's not a linear process, but it's certainly manageable and potentially lucrative.

This isn't an exhaustive guide, but it's certainly comprehensive enough to get you started on your path to creating a thriving short-term rental business. There is no one-size-fits-all strategy, so experimentation and adaptation will be key to your success. With time, practice, and patience, you'll eventually craft a formula that works perfectly for you and your property. Best of luck!

# Chapter 6. Optimizing Property Listings for Success

For the short-term rental marketplace, the first impression is often made digitally, via your property listing. This initial introduction, in essence, is a marketing pitch—a carefully constructed montage of photographs, descriptions, and compelling features. Therefore, it becomes crucial to understand and apply optimization techniques tailored to this domain.

## 6.1. Quality Imagery

Upon entering your listing, the first thing prospective guests encounter are the photos of your property. To maximise the appeal, make sure your photos tell a comprehensive and compelling story about your space.

It's recommended to hire a professional real estate photographer if your budget permits. They possess the skill set to capture your space in its best light. Their photos often highlight the aesthetics and mood of your space, making your listing more appealing.

If you are photographing the rental yourself, ensure you use a good quality camera, ample lighting, and capture multiple angles to provide a comprehensive view. Each room should have a minimum of three photographs. Don't forget to include photos of significant features such as excellent views, outdoor spaces, tech amenities (like smart TVs, home theatres), or luxurious bathrooms.

## 6.2. Compelling Title and Description

Title: Keep it short, attention-grabbing, and descriptive. Incorporate key elements like property type (e.g., "cozy cottage," "luxurious condo"), prominent features (e.g, "with stunning sea view"), or neighborhood attributes (e.g., "in heart of downtown").

Description: This is your chance to dive deeper into details. Start off with a catchy introduction, then break into bullet points exploring features, amenities, unique selling points, and general house rules. Always be honest and transparent about what your property can or can't offer. A floor plan can be beneficial for bigger properties. This allows guests to visualize walking through your space.

Consider using enticing language yet conveying the functional aspects too. For example: "Wake up to the soothing rhythm of ocean waves in our sea-view master bedroom equipped with a king-size Tempur-Pedic mattress."

## 6.3. Pricing Strategy and Dynamic Pricing

Your pricing should strive for a balance between attractiveness to guests and profitability. Too high might turn guests away, while too low might signify lesser quality or suspicious listing. Using Airbnb's Smart Pricing tool can be a starting point, but also research listings similar to your property around your location for a competitive quote.

A more refined strategy would include dynamic pricing. Here, you adjust prices based on factors such as demand, seasonality, and local events. Higher prices during peak season or local events and lower prices during off-peak times ensure your rental income remains optimized.

## 6.4. Amenities That Stand Out

Guests prioritize certain amenities above others. Adding amenities such as high-speed internet, a comfortable workspace, modern kitchen appliances, or luxurious beddings can make your listing more appealing. If you can provide unique amenities like a hot tub, pool, or rental bikes, make sure to highlight them—their mere presence may close the deal.

## 6.5. Instant Book Feature

The 'Instant Book' feature lists your property under searches for guests who want quick booking confirmation. Having this turned on can increase your visibility and subsequently your bookings. However, it also means skipping the pre-screening of guests. Hence, weigh the pros and cons before making a decision.

## 6.6. Responding to Reviews

Building a positive reputation is quintessential for success on Airbnb. Encourage guests to leave reviews and always respond to them—both the praise and criticisms. Thank reviewers who leave positive feedback and address negative criticisms promptly and professionally.

Repair any valid issues pointed out. This is not only good customer service but conveys to potential guests that you're committed to providing an excellent experience.

## 6.7. Superhost Status

Achieving the Airbnb Superhost status should be your goal. In addition to a badge next to your listing, benefits include better visibility in search results and priority customer support. The requirements for Superhost status include maintaining a high response rate, high overall rating, and complying with Airbnb's policies.

Optimizing your Airbnb property listing may require a significant amount of effort and attention-to-detail. However, it will pay off in the long run in the form of increased bookings, satisfied guests, lucrative revenue, and sustained growth of your short-term rental venture. Remember, success in the Airbnb domain is not an overnight miracle but the result of consistent efforts fueled by strategic insights and an unwavering focus on guest experience.

# Chapter 7. Financial Planning for your Airbnb Venture

Starting a venture in Airbnb requires strategic financial planning. The profitability of your short-term rental business largely depends on how well you manage your financial resources. This section presents a holistic guide to managing your capital, cash flows, and profitability of your Airbnb business.

## 7.1. Understanding your startup costs

No business starts without capital, and the Airbnb venture is no different. But how much does it indeed cost to start an Airbnb business? Here are the significant expenses you need to consider:

- Acquisition cost: This could either be the cost of buying a new property or the lease expense if you're renting the property.

- Renovations and repairs: The cost required to bring the property to rental market standards.

- Furnishing and decor: Investing in comfortable and appealing furnishings and decorations can make a significant difference in attracting guests.

- Professional services: These services include photography, legal advice, financial advice, and insurance coverage.

- Utility setup: Some properties may need additional utilities installed or updated.

Having a comprehensive list of the startup costs gives you a clear picture of how much capital you need to jumpstart your Airbnb venture.

# 7.2. Risk and ROI assessment

Assessing potential risks and the return on investment (ROI) is an integral part of your financial planning. Predominantly, your Airbnb business's ROI involves two variables: property price (your investment) and expected annual earnings.

ROI = ((Gain from investment - cost of investment) / cost of investment) * 100%

It's essential to calculate potential ROI ahead of time, considering factors like market trends, competition, demand, and location. Different locations attract different rental incomes. Therefore, knowing your potential earnings gives you a clear picture of your payback period and whether to proceed with the business or not.

When it comes to risk, you need to think about possible hurdles that could make running your business difficult or even impossible. These can be regulatory, such as changes in rental laws, or situational, like global pandemics, which could affect travel and hence the demand for short-term rentals.

# 7.3. Structuring your pricing

Deciding how much to charge your guests is a crucial step in financial planning. Price your rentals too high, and you'll turn away potential guests. Price them too low, and you'll be leaving money on the table.

A good pricing strategy for your Airbnb should factor in:

- Cost-based pricing: You should consider your costs (including overhead) and required profit margin to offer sustainable prices.
- Value-based pricing: Pricing according to the perceived value of your property from a guest's point of view.

- Competitor-based pricing: Considering what others in your neighborhood are charging for similar properties.

Implementing a dynamic pricing strategy where prices adjust based on demand (higher during peak seasons, lower during the off-peak) can also aid in maximizing your revenues.

# 7.4. Cash Flow Analysis

Just as with any other business, cash flow management is crucial for the success of an Airbnb venture. You must track your financial operations: money coming in from bookings and outgoing for expenses.

Understanding and anticipating your operational expenses, seasonal fluctuation in revenues, and unexpected costs and planning for these uncertainties helps maintain positive cash flow. It's also important to keep an emergency fund to handle surprise expenses, unseen repairs, or a sudden drop in demand.

# 7.5. Accounting and Taxation

Proper accounting is essential not only for financial management but also to adhere to the regulatory requirements. Some expenses are tax-deductible, and understanding these helps decrease your tax liability.

Depreciation, insurance, cleaning, property fees, the commission payable to Airbnb, and more are considered operational costs that can be deducted from your rental income, reducing your overall tax burden.

Teaming up with a professional accountant who understands the nuances of the short-term rental business can be a wise move to handle accounting and taxation efficiently and effectively.

## 7.6. Profitability

Finally, achieve profitability by managing your revenues and costs effectively. Remember to recalculate your ROI periodically as situations change, and always look out for the ideal balance of providing great guest experiences and managing costs. Make it a routine to assess your financial performance and make necessary adjustments in pricing, cost management, and more.

Remember, wealth creation in Airbnb is not an overnight process but a gradual journey that demands patience, strategic financial planning, and sound decisions.

# Chapter 8. Dealing with Challenges in the Airbnb Business

Operating a successful Airbnb business isn't always a walk in the park. There are myriad challenges that can arise, which demand flexibility, resilience, and strategic thinking. We will extensively analyze these challenges in this section and give you effective strategies to deal with them, maximizing your wealth creation prospects in short-term rentals.

## 8.1. Regulatory Hurdles

As the short-term rental business gains popularity, governments around the world are actively developing regulations to govern it. These rules vary – from location to location, and from time to time – and may include obtaining relevant permits, paying certain taxes, abiding by zoning laws, or even outright bans on short-term rentals.

Understanding these laws and the potential implications for your business should be your first step towards setting up a thriving Airbnb business. You may need to enlist the help of professionals, such as attorneys or town planners, to unravel complex regulatory issues.

Remember, ignorance of the law is not bliss in business, it's a potential nightmare. Violations can result in hefty fines, lawsuits, or the end of your Airbnb enterprise entirely. Thus, keeping up-to-date with the ever-evolving regulatory landscape is paramount to your business's long-term survival and prosperity.

## 8.2. Managing Your Property and Guests

Managing multiple properties or even one property can pose logistical challenges particularly if you're juggling it with other responsibilities. Tasks such as cleaning, maintenance, stocking supplies, and managing bookings can quickly become a burden.

Tools such as property management software come in handy in streamlining these tasks. You can schedule cleanings, organize bookings, and manage communications with guests through these platforms.

In addition, outsourcing tasks is another feasible approach to handle the load effectively. Hiring cleaners or a property manager to handle the day-to-day operations allows you to focus on other strategic aspects of your business.

Customer service is crucial too. Negative guest experiences can quickly spell doom for your Airbnb venture, demolishing your reputation. Be agile in addressing concerns—respond promptly to messages or calls, fix issues, and ensure your guests have a smooth, comfortable stay.

## 8.3. Dealing with Bad Guests

Whilst most guests have good intentions, occasionally, you might encounter 'bad guests.' They could damage your property, disregard house rules, or create disturbances that upset your neighbors.

A solid line of defense is a thorough screening process. Understanding who you're renting to can help mitigate potential risks. Check their previous reviews, validate their identity, and trust your gut instincts.

Having a clear, comprehensive set of house rules can also help maintain decorum. Ensure that these rules are instantly visible to the prospective renters, and make them understand the potential consequences of breaking any rules.

However, if a guest does cause problems, being prepared to resolve disputes amicably and, when necessary, involve Airbnb's resolution center will help you secure your interests.

## 8.4. Navigating Market Fluctuations

The Airbnb business is subject to market dynamics. Seasonal swings, changes in tourism trends, economic fluctuations, and global crises (such as the COVID-19 pandemic) can sharply hit demand and rates.

To cushion your business from these shocks, consider diversifying your guest base. Market your property for more extended stays or attract non-tourist guests—like business travelers or locals looking for a short-term rental.

Diversify your portfolio too. Owning or managing properties in different markets spreads your risks, helping insulate your business from localized downturns.

And importantly, remain adaptable. Be ready to change rates in line with demand and market conditions, offer enticing deals during low seasons, and beef up your marketing efforts when needed.

## 8.5. Conclusion

In business, challenges are not stumbling blocks but stepping stones to better strategies and greater success. Understanding potential challenges in the Airbnb business helps prepare for them, giving you a leg up over an unprepared competition. By staying updated on regulations, effectively managing your property, wisely navigating market fluctuations, and dealing with the occasional bad guest, you can face these hurdles with confidence and guarantee your Airbnb business's longevity and profitability.

Note that this chapter does not exhaust the gamut of potential challenges nor their solutions. It's crucial to continually learn, adapt, stay up-to-date with industry changes, network with other Airbnb hosts, and remain open to new ideas and strategies to handle possible disruptions effectively. As Hall of Fame quarterback Roger Staubach once said, "Spectacular achievements are always preceded by unspectacular preparation."

# Chapter 9. Maximizing Profit: Pricing and Value Addition Techniques

The pursuit of profit maximization in any business is akin to the dance of a tightrope walker. In the short-term rental business like Airbnb, understanding the sweet spot between affordable pricing and premium value addition is of the utmost importance.

## 9.1. Understanding Your Market

The first step in maximizing profit in the short-term rental arena is to understand your market deeply. Be very knowledgeable of your competition; their listings, prices, and value-added features. This will give you an edge in setting your own pricing model.

To effect this, make a comprehensive list of all competing listings within your vicinity and their various features. List them in a tabular form for ease of reference.

| Listing | Price per Night | Features |
| --- | --- | --- |
| Listing A | $150 | Pool, Wi-Fi, Secure Parking |
| Listing B | $100 | Wi-Fi, Free Breakfast |
| Listing C | $175 | Pool, Wi-Fi, Secure Parking, Free Breakfast |

From the information gathered, you can make smart pricing decisions that give you a competitive edge and maximize your profit.

# 9.2. How to Set Your Prices

The price you set for your listing is directly tied to the value you're offering. Setting competitive prices while ensuring consistent profit growth can be achieved through dynamic pricing strategies.

Dynamic pricing is not just an abstract concept; it's about adjusting your prices according to market demands. Times of high demand should reflect in your pricing. Additionally, consider the time of the week, seasonality, and even hours of the day.

To illustrate, a studio apartment in a city's central business district would likely see a surge in bookings during weekdays because of business travellers, while the weekends might attract a different clientele with different price sensitivities. Similarly, a cottage by the beach would probably be in high demand during summer and holiday periods.

# 9.3. Value Addition

Offering additional value to your guests is a proven strategy for boosting profits. Analyze and understand what amenities or services your guests appreciate the most, then find ways to provide or enhance them. These additions might range from providing superfast Wi-Fi to offering dedicated workspace or adding premium entertainment options.

Such amenities may necessitate a small investment initially but the returns in terms of bookings and pricing can compensate for that. Consider the following comparison table:

| Amenity | Cost | Potential increase in bookings |
|---|---|---|
| Superfast Wi-Fi | $20 extra per month | 20% |

| Amenity | Cost | Potential increase in bookings |
|---|---|---|
| Dedicated workspace | $150 one-time cost | 15% |
| Premium entertainment options | $30 per month | 10% |

From the above table, investing an extra $20 per month on Superfast Wi-Fi could potentially increase your bookings by 20%.

## 9.4. Incentivizing Longer Stays

Encouraging guests to book for longer periods is another effective way to maximize profit. Discounts for longer stays are often a good draw for many guests. You can offer a decreasing scale of discounts for weekly and monthly stays.

| Duration of Stay | Discount | 1 Week |
|---|---|---|
| 10% | 2 Weeks | 15% |

Longer stays mean less turnover in terms of cleaning and preparation for new guests, thus saving you money in terms of maintenance costs.

## 9.5. Professional Photography

In the era of digital marketing, making a stellar first impression is vital. Professional, high-quality photos can set a listing apart from hundreds of others available on the platform.

Investment in quality photography may seem like an added cost, but consider it as an improvement to your listing's online "curb appeal." The better the presentation of your listing, the more it will attract potential guests and stand out from the crowd, allowing you to charge a premium.

## 9.6. The Art of Upselling

An effective technique to maximize profit after securing a booking is through upselling or offering additional services for a fee. You might offer airport pickup and drop-off service, guided tours, or grocery delivery. Although not every guest will avail of these services, those who do will increase your profits.

## 9.7. Learning from Reviews

And, last but not the least, always heed to your client feedback. Reviews from your guests can be insightful for your Airbnb business. Chances are they've stayed at other places in the past, and their inputs might contain ideas to improve your listing or affirm things that you're doing right. Continue doing what guests love and look to improve things they think you could do better.

Maximizing profits in the Airbnb business requires a blend of market intelligence, strategic pricing, value addition, and excellent customer service. By mastering these aspects, you can make your way to becoming a thriving short-term rental entrepreneur.

# Chapter 10. Real Stories, Real Success: Case Studies

Airbnb's platform revolutionized the lodging industry, inspiring hosts from around the globe to establish successful short-term rental businesses. Below are four inspiring real-life stories illustrating how ordinary people have made a significant financial impact through Airbnb.

## 10.1. The Abundant Beach House: Turning Passion into Profit

Jason and Carla, a Canadian couple, were retired and had a keen interest in the hospitality business. They started by leasing their already purchased beach house in the picturesque town of Tofino, British Columbia. Their house, with a lovely sea view and surrounded by nature, was perfect for holiday rentals.

They started by listing their home on Airbnb to test the waters. With some insightful interior design, a comprehensive guidebook for guests, and exceptional hospitality, their listing started getting booked consistently. The income generated was enough to cover their expenses with extra profit. Encouraged by their newfound success, they got a second beach-facing property and started managing both full-time. Now, they own and manage four properties, with annual earnings exceeding $200,000.

## 10.2. City Living: Transforming Spaces into Income

An interior designer Sofia from New York City had always a knack for creating captivating and Instagram-worthy spaces. She learned about the potential of Airbnb and decided to put her skills to use. She began by renting out her loft-style apartment in the heart of the bustling city, ensuring it was meticulously appointed to attract modern, trendy guests.

She later identified smaller rental properties that were less appealing, rented them, implemented striking and cost-efficient design improvements, and sub-let through Airbnb. Sofia didn't own these properties, yet her unique business model was cash-positive. Today, she manages ten listings in NYC, pulling in over $120,000 in annual profit.

## 10.3. Vanessa's Country Cabins: Hospitality Gone Rural

Vanessa, a wildlife enthusiast from Montana, transformed her passion for the outdoors into a lucrative Airbnb business. She converted two of her unused rustic cabins into guest houses, providing a cozy rural experience for travelers.

Beyond just the stay itself, Vanessa added unique 'experience' offerings, such as guided hiking, wildlife spotting, and home-cooked meals from locally sourced ingredients. Her Airbnb venture started generating a significant income, leading Vanessa to add more cabins to her listing and recruit her first employees. Today, she turns over more than $150,000 per annum from her cabin rentals.

## 10.4. Move Over Hotels: Boutique Accommodation Business with Airbnb

When Saeed from Dubai identified a gap in the market for boutique setups in locations with potential for high tourist influxes, he seized the opportunity. He purchased old properties, refurbished them with a modern Arabesque design flair, and listed his spaces on Airbnb.

His venture's initial success grew when he focused on providing stellar service, partnering with local tour agencies for recommendations, and using digital marketing strategies to boost visibility. With a current portfolio of 20 properties, his estimated annual income from Airbnb exceeds $400,000.

These 'real stories, real success' case studies illuminate the sky-high potential of Airbnb. Every host's journey is different, but they share common themes: seizing opportunities, providing exceptional hospitality, and continuously adapting to market dynamics. These hosts started by simply renting out a spare room or vacant property, and with their ingenuity and proactive efforts, transformed it into a thriving Airbnb business. Following their best practices, anyone can venture into the Airbnb market and achieve a comparable degree of success.

# Chapter 11. Future Trends in Short-term Rentals and Airbnb

The ever-evolving nature of the short-term rental market, spearheaded by platforms such as Airbnb, is underpinned by a plethora of factors including technological advancements, changes in traveler behavior, and shifts in regulatory landscapes. As we venture into this exciting new era, understanding these trends will be vital to capitalizing on opportunities and overcoming potential challenges.

## 11.1. Technological Advancements and Their Impact

The transformative power of technology is significant in the short-term rental industry. This is evident in the numerous advancements that have streamlined operations and enhanced user experiences.

One crucial technological trend is the rise of property management software. These platforms simplify the management of listings on multiple rental sites, automate tasks like guest communication and cleaning schedules, and provide financial reporting tools. Advanced analytics capabilities can also enable hosts to optimize pricing and occupancy rates.

Artificial Intelligence (AI) and machine learning are increasingly integrated into these technologies. They have the potential to provide predictive insights about market trends and personalized recommendations targeting guests' preferences. They're also powering smart home devices, enhancing the guest experience with next-level automation and security.

## 11.2. Consumer Behavior Shifts

Changes in travel and accommodation preferences profoundly affect the short-term rental market. Notably, there has been a growing preference for authentic local experiences over conventional hotels. More travelers are seeking homes that provide a sense of connection with the local culture. This trend towards experiential travel has driven hosts to offer not just a place to stay, but also unique local experiences.

Additionally, the surge in remote work and digital nomadism is reshaping accommodation needs. With an ability to work from anywhere, more people are taking advantage of extended stays in rental properties. Therefore, hosts need to furnish listings facilitating long-term stays, including workspace amenities and solid Wi-Fi.

## 11.3. Regulatory Evolution

As the popularity of platforms like Airbnb increases, regulatory frameworks around the world are evolving. Changes range from new tax obligations to operating licenses and zoning laws. The legal landscape is complex and varies from one jurisdiction to another, making compliance a critical factor for hosts. Those who proactively adapt to these changes can avoid penalties and leverage opportunities to differentiate themselves.

## 11.4. Green and Sustainable Tourism

The increasing consciousness towards the environment and sustainability is another influential trend. Guests are more likely to choose accommodations with eco-friendly practices. In response, hosts can improve their property's environmental footprint through energy-efficient appliances, recycling facilities, and other green initiatives.

# 11.5. Rise of Professional Hosting

The professionalization of short-term rentals is undeniably on the horizon. With the growing competition, a casual approach may no longer cut it. Successful hosts are treating their Airbnb listings as a full-fledged business, focusing on guest experiences, investment in quality furniture and amenities, professional photography, and active online marketing.

In conclusion, the volatile nature of trends means that they can shift rapidly, especially in such a dynamic field. By keeping up-to-date with the latest technology, consumer preferences, regulatory changes, sustainability practices, and business strategies, hosts can not only navigate but leverage these trends to create a successful short-term rental business. As the industry continues to evolve, those who can anticipate and adapt to these trends will be the ones to thrive in the challenging yet exciting world of short-term rentals and Airbnb.

While forecasting future trends can never be precise, this report provides an insight into the plausible directions of the Airbnb and short-term rental markets. Armed with these insights, hosts can foster a robust and resilient business model that ensures profitability today and scales with the tides of tomorrow.

www.ingramcontent.com/pod-product-compliance
Lightning Source LLC
Chambersburg PA
CBHW071049260726
48661CB00007B/3229